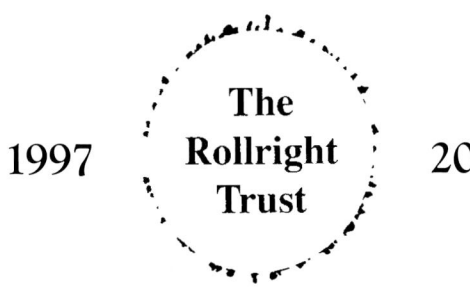

1997 **The Rollright Trust** 20

CW01024425

An Illustrated Guide to The Rollright Stones

By George Lambrick

*In Memory of Dohn Prout, Site Manager 2000-2007
through whose energy the amenity of the Stones was transformed*

The Rollright Trust

2017

Table of Contents

Introduction

The Rollright Stones consist of three megalithic monuments dating from different periods:

- An early Neolithic burial chamber, The Whispering Knights c. 3,800-3,500 BC

- A late Neolithic ceremonial stone circle, The King's Men c. 2,500-2000 BC

- A standing stone , the King Stone, probably mid Bronze Age c. 1,800-1,500 BC

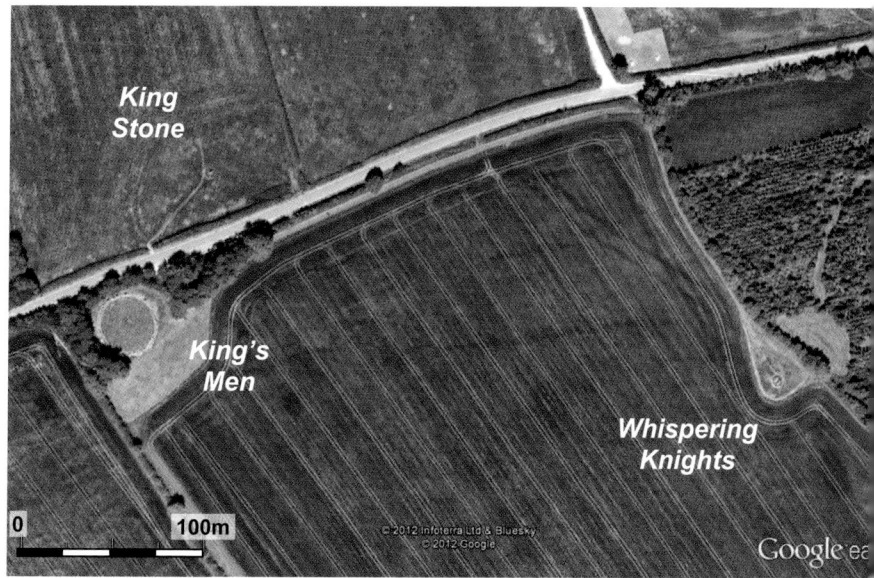

The Stones are located on a ridge that forms the northern edge of the Cotswold Hills and is the watershed between the River Severn flowing west and the River Thames flowing east. There are especially fine views northwest over the village of Long Compton towards the Vale of Moreton, the Stour valley and outlying parts of the Cotswolds (below). The road bisecting the complex is an ancient salt way, now the boundary of Oxfordshire and Warwickshire.

The King's Men

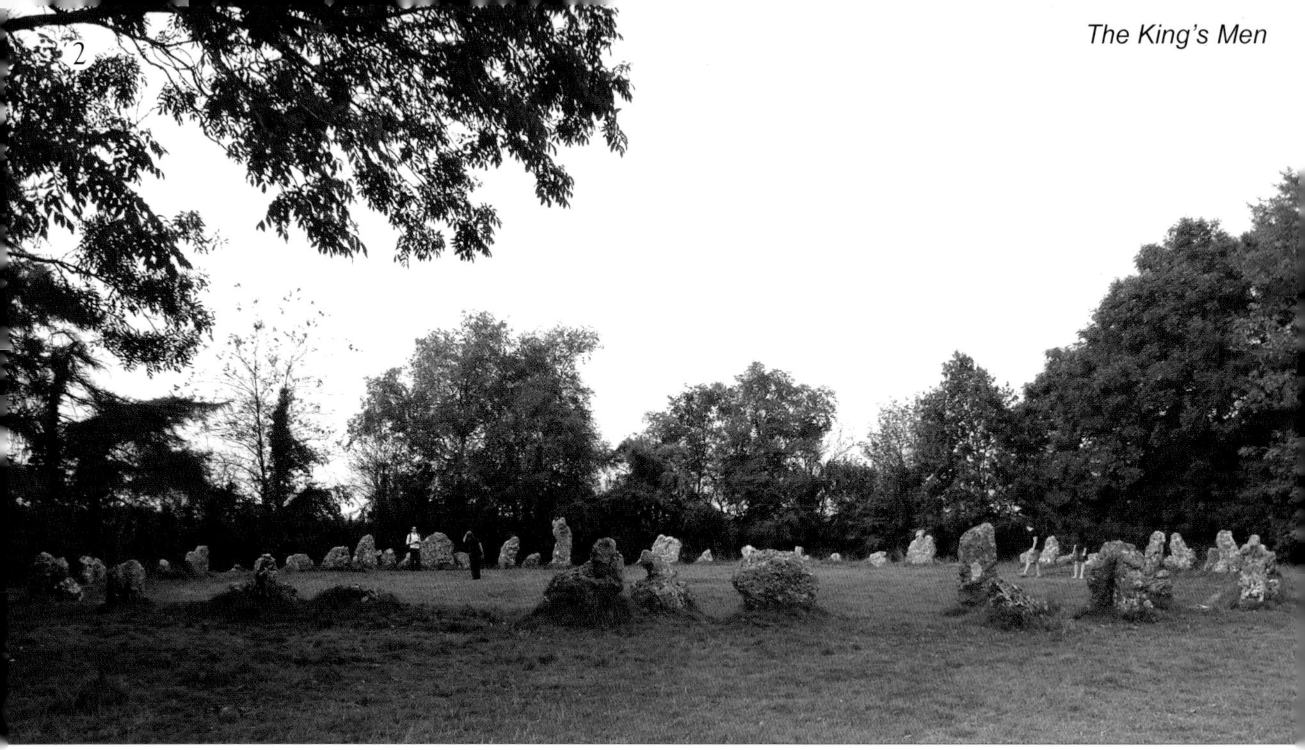

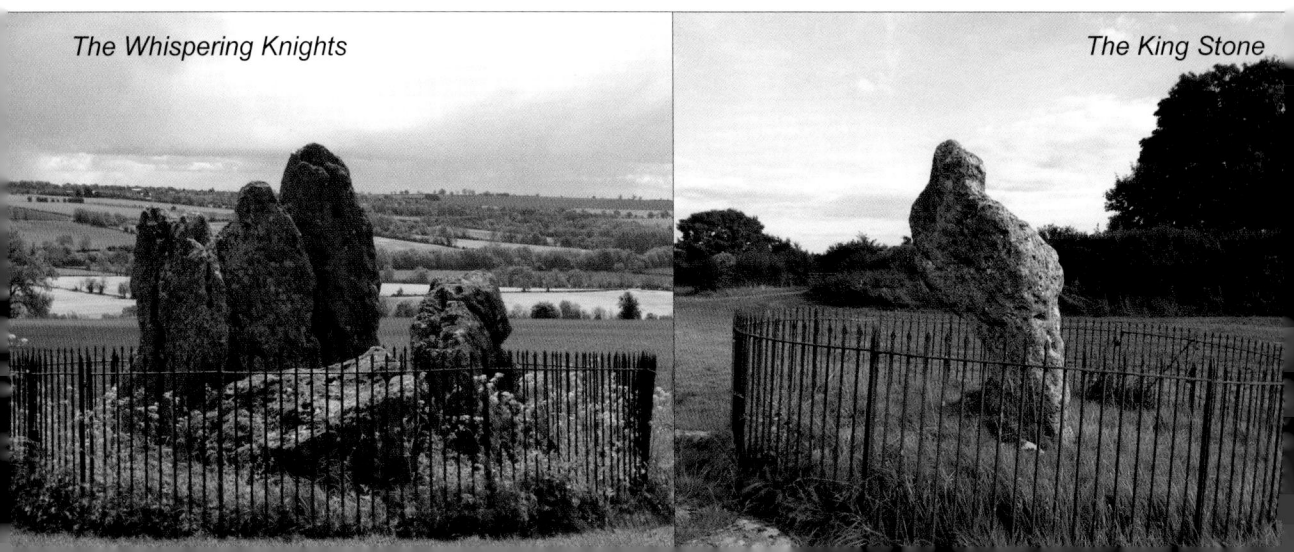

Apart from the Stones themselves, the complex includes several other ancient remains (right):

1 Possible former Neolithic barrow and burial chamber (destroyed) c. 4000-3500 BC?
2 Site of Bronze Age round barrow c. 1700BC
3 Bronze Age cairn c. 2000-1800BC
4 Site of possible barrow
5 Late Bronze Age or early Iron Age trackway and field boundary c. 700-500 BC
6 Iron Age farming settlement c. 300-100 BC
7 Saxon cemetery c. 500-700 AD

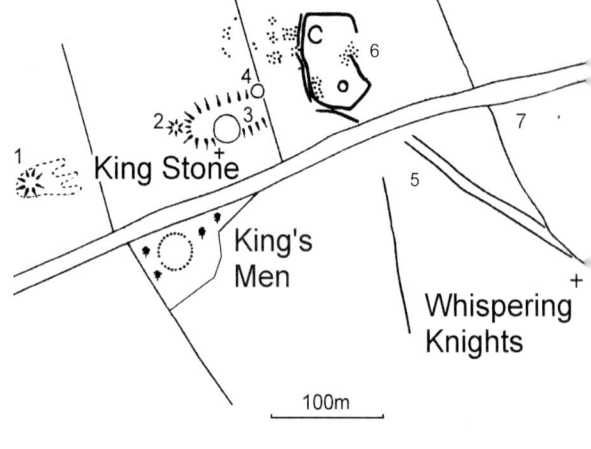

The Whispering Knights

The King Stone

Myths and Legends

The Rollright Stones are associated with a rich variety of folklore traditions, some over 400 years old. They include a petrifaction and witchcraft legend; the stones being uncountable; various animation stories (eg the stones going down the hill to drink, fortune telling); and bad luck stories.

The Stones take their names from a legend about a king and his army who were marching over the Cotswolds when they met a witch who challenged the king saying, *"Seven long strides shalt thou take and if Long Compton thou canst see, King of England thou shalt be"*. On his seventh stride a mound rose up obscuring the view, and the witch turned them all to stone: the king became the King Stone; his army the King's Men; and his knights the Whispering Knights (plotting treachery). The witch became an elder tree, supposedly still in a nearby hedge: if the elder is cut the spell is broken and the Stones will come back to life.

As with some Welsh standing stones, it is said that any passing carrier who chips bits off the King Stone will return to his cart only to find the wheels are irrevocably locked!

Other stories include the Stones being sources of fertility and acting as oracles.

A local farmer supposedly took one of the largest stones to make a bridge over a stream. It took 24 horses to drag the stone down the hill and a man was killed on the way. Eventually they got the stone across the stream, but by morning it had flipped over onto the bank! This happened each time they replaced it; then the crops failed.... So the farmer decided he had better put the stone back, and it only took one horse to drag it up the hill!

By tradition the stones of the King's Men are uncountable: if you count them three times and get the same number at each attempt you can have any wish you like! (It is harder than you might expect). It is said that a baker once tried to count them by placing buns on each stone, but some had gone missing when he collected them up.

Changing Ideas about the Stones

The Rollright Stones are first referred to in a text of late 12th century origin, *De Mirabilibus Britanniae* (*On the Wonders of Britain*). The latin entry (right) reads *"In the region of Oxfordshire there are great stones disposed as if by the hand of man. But at what time, or by what people, or for what memorial or significance this was done is not known. However that place is called Rollendrich by the local people"*

  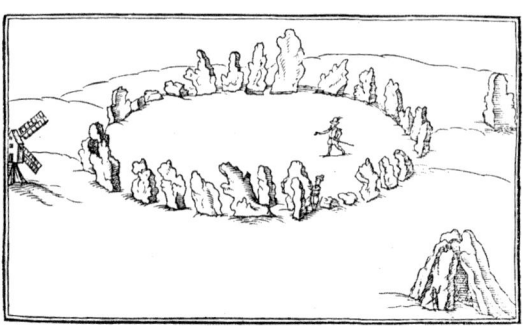 

John Leland mentioned the Stones in his *Itinerary* (1538-42), and the earliest depiction of them is in the tapestry maps of Warwickshire and Worcestershire commissioned in the 1590s by Ralph Sheldon of Weston (above left). The earliest description of the Stones was by William Camden, who attributed them to the Danes in his great account of antiquities, *Britannia* (1586), of which the 1607 edition gives the first printed illustration (above right).

By 1649 the Oxford antiquary, John Aubrey (above left) was suggesting that such monuments might be pre-Roman. A decade or so later, inspired by Thomas Browne's *Urn Burial* (1658), Ralph Sheldon (the younger) unsuccessfully looked for burials in the stone circle. Dr Robert Plot (above centre), first curator of the Ashmolean Museum and Secretary of the Royal Society, gave a detailed account of the Stones in his *Natural History of Oxfordshire* (1677). He favoured the Danish attribution, comparing them with Scandinavian megaliths. His illustration of the Stones by Michael Burghers (right) is a remarkably accurate bird's eye view (see p.9).

John Aubrey's suggestion that stone monuments like Rollright might be pre-Roman was a vitally important insight, coming almost 200 years before archaeologists divided prehistory into the now familiar technological ages of Stone, Bronze and Iron. Since such megalithic monuments were clearly religious and ceremonial structures, and Julius Caesar had described the Druids as being the priestly class of Britons, it was logical to attribute them to the Druids. This view was enthusiastically taken up by William Stukeley (left), the leading antiquary of his day, who visited Rollright in 1710 and 1724.

Stukeley was a good field archaeologist and he identified two barrows and a long mound close to the King Stone which he thought was a burial monument (top). Obsessed by Druids, he suggested that the King Stone was where the Archdruid conducted ceremonies, and the long mound his burial place. He asked his friend Henry Gale to measure the Stone circle — and then claimed that the diameter fitted a whole number of his 'Druid's Cubits'.

The Stones were now firmly prehistoric, and few important new insights emerged in the following hundred years.

But in 1804, during a tour recording the architecture of local churches, Thomas Fisher produced a valuable set of drawings and watercolours of the Stones, including the King's Men (upper right) and the barrow with displaced stones west of the King Stone, first seen by Stukeley (bottom right). He records it as being 'undermined' — probably due to agricultural clearance. It has since disappeared altogether.

In the early 19th century, the former common land of Long Compton was enclosed and the road past the Stones upgraded. Quarries were dug alongside the road to provide stone for walls and road metalling, and Thomas Beesley reported that in 1836 and again in 1854 such work had led to the discovery of pottery, bones 'of men and horses,' burnt stones, human skeletons and other finds. These are almost certainly a mixture of material from an Iron Age enclosure and, as he correctly observed, a Saxon cemetery (see p.14 and p.15).

By then archaeology was becoming more scientific, with the chronology for prehistory being divided into the Stone, Bronze and Iron Ages that still provide a general purpose timescale today. There was also growing interest in possible associations of megalithic monuments with astronomical alignments. The solar astronomer Sir Norman Lockyer visited and surveyed the King's Men in 1868 and 1873, and in 1905 annotated his initial drawing (left) to show changes arising from the site's 'restoration' when it was included in the first Ancient Monuments Act in 1882.

The Rollright Stones were popularised by the photographer Henry Taunt (below right), and the amateur archaeologist H. M. J. Underhill who painted his own lantern slides for public lectures (below left). Reflecting other preoccupations of the day, the folklore of the Stones was reviewed in 1895 by Arthur Evans (later the excavator of Knossos in Crete).

The Whispering Knights

The Whispering Knights is considered to be the oldest of the Rollright monuments, a 'portal dolmen' burial chamber probably of the early Neolithic period dating from about 3,800 to 3,500 BC.

Its façade, mimicking a 'portal' or doorway (top right), faces downhill (perhaps the direction from which the tomb was approached). These impressive stones — together with three or four missing ones — would have been crowned by the large capstone (now fallen). The chamber would have been accessed through a gap behind the portal.

Funerary customs at this period involved interaction with the bones of ancestors, placing and re-arranging them within the chamber. The monument was probably used periodically over very many centuries. Pottery dating from the early and late Neolithic and early Bronze Age has been found in the immediate vicinity, and a human bone probably washed out of the chamber has been radiocarbon dated c. 1520-1414 BC (middle Bronze Age).

The stones were moved and raised using only sledges, rollers, levers and ropes. It might have taken 60 people to erect the huge western portal stone. The capstone may have been hauled up split log 'rails' set in stones heaped up inside and behind the chamber: traces of such stones survive round the base of the chamber and they may have been used to form a low kidney-shaped platform cairn, like other tombs of this type (suggested by a patch of rubble preserved beneath the modern ploughsoil — right) leaving the tall portal and massive capstone impressively monumental. The soil beneath these stones indicates that the tomb may have been erected in woodland.

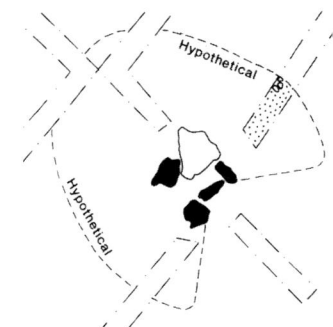

Other comparable burial chambers in this part of the Cotswolds include the Hoar Stone at Enstone (bottom right); a chambered barrow at Adlestrop; possibly one at Churchill; and perhaps the ruinous barrow west of the King Stone recorded by Fisher (see p.5).

The King's Men

The King's Men stone circle is later than the Whispering Knights — perhaps by more than a thousand years. The circle was probably built in the later Neolithic period around 2,500 BC. It was positioned due west of the earlier burial chamber, just off the crest of the ridge on ground sloping slightly to the south.

The stone circle would have been used for ceremonial gatherings. It is circular, about 32m across. The various legends noted earlier (p.3) reflect the fact that many stones have gone missing, probably taken for building material. But the original entrance opposite the tallest stone still survives, marked by two 'portal' stones just outside the line of the main ring, one of which is now fallen (below centre, bottom). This north-north-west to south-south-east axis through the entrance is not thought to be significant astronomically, but may suggest that the formal approach was from the valley.

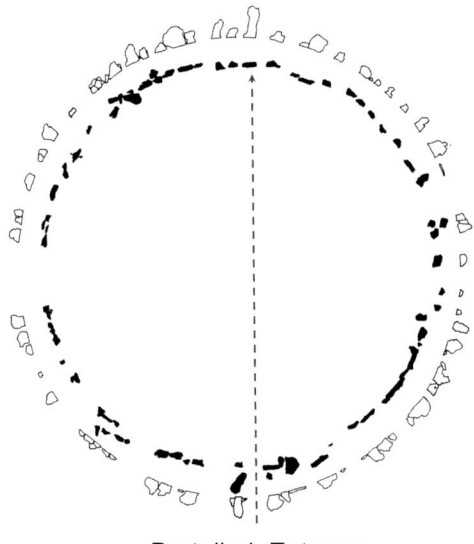

Portalled Entrance

The stones are surface boulders derived from the local limestone and have not been shaped. Stukeley described them as *'corroded like worm eaten wood'*. Some have naturally eroded holes through them (see p.19). The tallest stone has a shield carved on it that may date from the 17th or 18th century (far left).

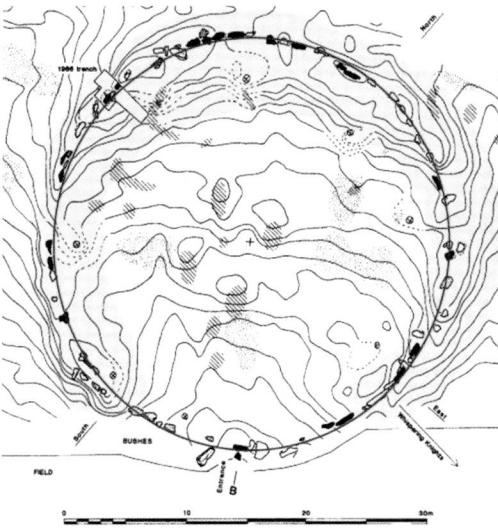

In 1882 several fallen stones were re-erected, but a comparison with old drawings (above) reveals which ones are unchanged since the 17th century. This shows that the ring was more accurately circular than it now appears, and suggests that the largest stones may have been positioned opposite the entrance either side of the tallest stone. Some may have been placed with their smoother sides facing inwards. Several undisturbed stones (notably four near the tallest stone) are almost touching, suggesting that originally the ring was continuous except for the one narrow entrance. Excavation in 1986 revealed two close-set original stone-holes where one of the missing stones once stood and another had been re-erected (bottom left).

A detailed contour survey (centre right) shows that the stones are embanked, probably made by levelling the interior of the circle, leaving a 20 m wide gap corresponding with the orientation of the entrance. Four low mounds near the centre with corresponding pits revealed by geophysics may be 19th century tree planting holes.

Stone circles of this distinctive form — with many closely spaced stones, a portalled entrance, embanked and with a levelled interior — differ from most others in Britain except for a distinct group in the Lake District (like Swinside below) and a few in Ireland and Wales. Thus the people who built the King's Men probably had connections with such areas.

Sunken Kirk, Swinside, Cumbria

The King Stone

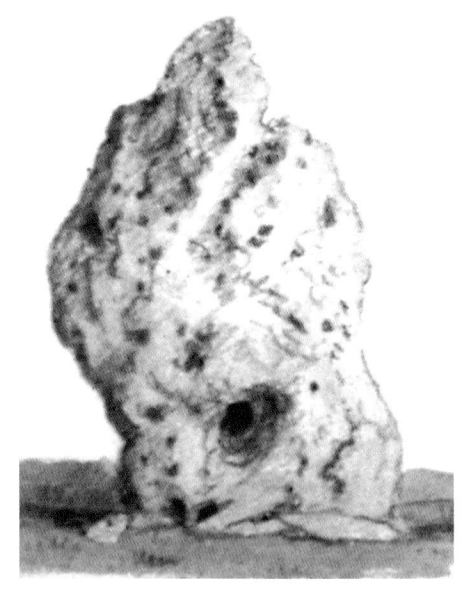

There have been many theories about the origin and function of the King Stone. Early antiquaries saw it as marking the place of assembly for a Danish King or an Archdruid; or the sole remaining stone in an avenue leading to the King's Men like the West Kennet Avenue at Avebury. It has also been interpreted as an astronomically aligned outlier of the stone circle, or as a guide post marking the location of the Stones for travellers. But none of these ideas stands up to scrutiny.

Nor was it part of a Neolithic long cairn (putatively the long mound that supposedly rose up to block the King's view of Long Compton). Writing about Cotswold barrows in the 1920s, O. G. S. Crawford had suggested that it was one half of a 'porthole' entrance to a burial chamber (the other half formed by a missing similar hollow-sided stone). But comparison with Thomas Fisher's drawing of 1804 (top) and a photograph of 1904 shows that the large bite out of the eastern side of the King (right) was entirely the result of 19th century souvenir hunting.

Excavations in the 1980s (left) revealed a hitherto unknown Bronze Age stone burial cairn near the King Stone and the small round barrow first recorded by Stukeley just to the west. A circular ditch nearby revealed by geophysics and two others known from air photos beyond the King's Men, may also be barrows. Both the excavated sites revealed cremation burials that had been marked by wooden posts (see p.11-12).

As with some other standing stones, it is thus likely that the King Stone was erected as a permanent memorial, demarcating the burial ground as a sacred place.

The King Stone Barrows:
The Round Cairn

The long mound that supposedly hid the view of Long Compton from the legendary King is not a long barrow but a natural knoll. Nonetheless, this prominent position was chosen as the location for a circular burial cairn (bottom left; cf p.18). It was 17m across, built of stones heaped round a central burial chamber, of which the tip of the capstone is just visible in the grass. Neat dry stone walling formed the edge of the cairn (bottom right).

The central chamber was not investigated, but secondary cremations were found in the top of the cairn (left). Close to the King Stone another cremation dated to c.1735-1713 BC had been marked by an upright post (below right) and a cremated child's tooth with charcoal radiocarbon dated to c.1925-1728 BC was found where the dry stone walling had been burnt (bottom right).

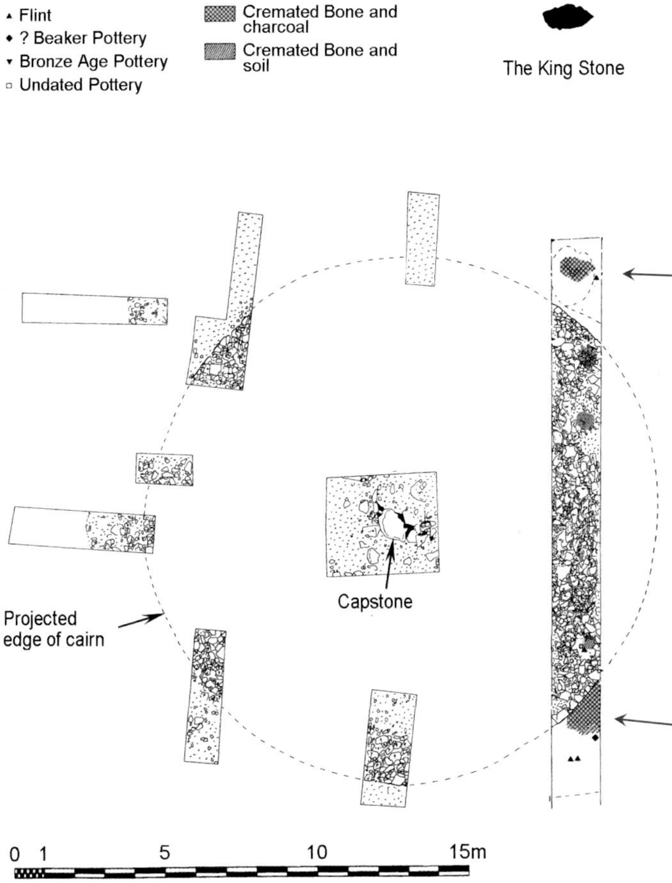

▲ Flint
◆ ? Beaker Pottery
▼ Bronze Age Pottery
▢ Undated Pottery

Cremated Bone and charcoal
Cremated Bone and soil

The King Stone

Capstone

Projected edge of cairn

0 1   5   10   15m

The King Stone Barrows:
The Small Barrow

In the eighteenth century Stukeley identified a small barrow north-west of the King Stone (top left, C). The mound had since been flattened by ploughing, leaving only a scatter of stones overlying a thin layer of original soil (left).

Excavation in the 1980s revealed various human cremation deposits, including an unusual 'tunnel' cremation radiocarbon dated to c.1880-1746 BC that had been marked by a large, roughly rectangular post (bottom right). Close to the foot of the post at around 1731-1719 or 1692-1500 BC, the cremated remains of a child were buried with an upturned collared urn in a small pit (below left).

The 'tunnel' cremation consisted of a mixture of cremated bone and charcoal placed in a small cave-like hole hollowed out of the side of a rock-cut pit. A small blocking stone had been placed vertically across the entrance of the void and the large post was then placed in the pit. The remainder of the cremated bone and charcoal was scattered round the base of the post before its pit was filled in with well-packed soil and stones to hold the post upright.

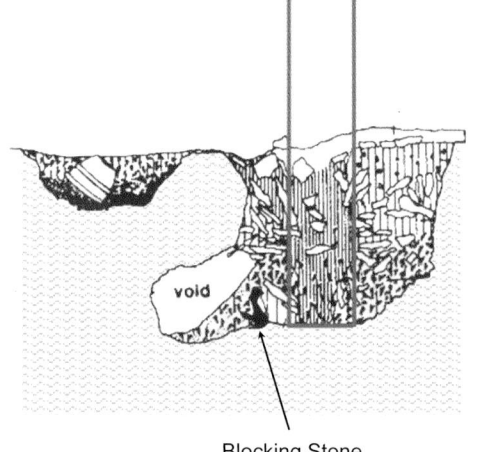

Blocking Stone

Activity Revealed by Worked Stone

Excavation of the buried soil beneath the small barrow near the King Stone (centre left, right) revealed a small, dense scatter of late Mesolithic flints (c.6,500-4,000 BC). Apart from a broken arrowhead, they were all snapped bladelets (top right). None of them joined, suggesting that they were discards, the other halves having been taken away to make implements. They were found next to a tree-throw hole where a fallen tree may have created a small glade that was a convenient place to prepare the flints — a task that perhaps **took just minutes.**

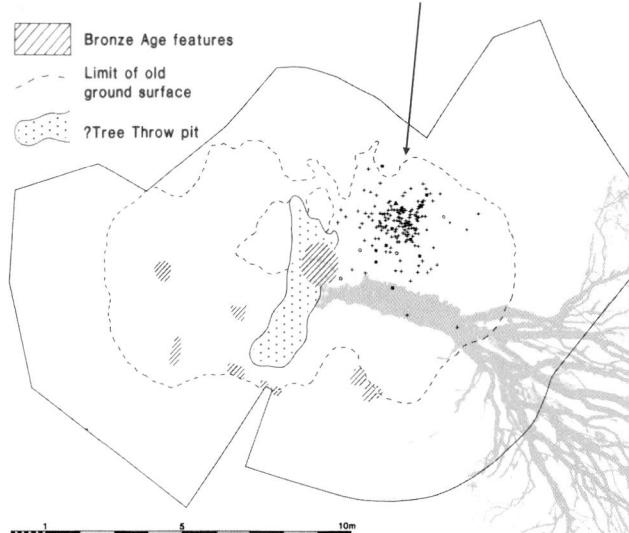

The distribution of worked stone from fields near the Stones shows how the area recurrently attracted people for over 4,000 years from the late Mesolithic to the Bronze Age. The finds were densest off the crest of the ridge but above the spring line, and thinned out noticeably about 500m east of the Stones (below left). The finds include a large flint core, probably from the Berkshire Downs 40 km away (below right), and a greenstone axe from Cornwall.

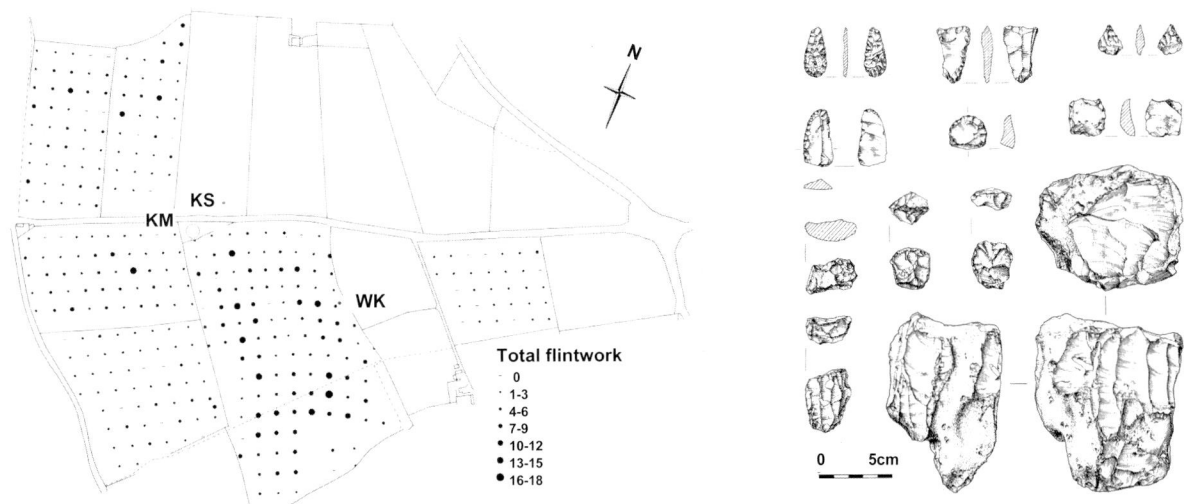

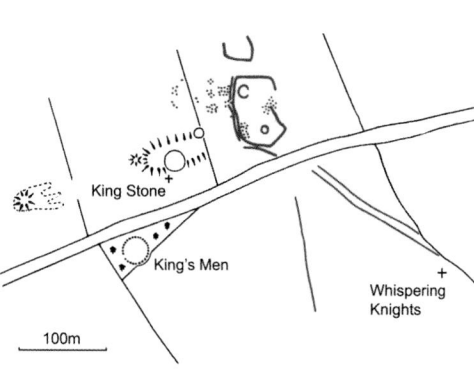

Late Prehistoric Farmers

A trackway and single field ditch in the field between the Whispering Knights and the King's Men are visible on air photographs (see top left and p.1). Pottery from small-scale excavations suggest that the ditches are part of a late Bronze Age or early Iron Age field system c.1000-500 BC. North of the road, a later ditched enclosure known from air photography and geophysical survey (centre left) is located on the line of the trackway. A small trench (bottom left) revealed only middle Iron Age occupation, though the settlement might have had earlier origins.

The enclosure ditch (top right) was rock-cut, almost 2m deep. The stone from it may have been used to build a wall to deter rustlers (or impress neighbours). A shallow sub-circular ditch in the northwest corner of the enclosure may have surrounded a house. Outside the enclosure, rock-cut pits (bottom right) were probably used for grain storage. Animal bones and carbonised remains of crops and weeds indicate a typical mixed farm growing spelt wheat and rearing sheep, cattle and a few pigs.

In the Roman period a new agricultural settlement was established west of the King Stone, a thin scatter of pottery showing that the surrounding fields were manured. At the King's Men pieces of pottery have been found, suggesting that the Stones were visited in the Roman period.

Saxon Cemetery and Meeting Place

Prehistoric monuments were often recognised as special places by pagan Anglo-Saxon communities who settled in Britain in the 5th and 6th centuries AD. Rollright was no exception. The Stones lie within the area of Saxon settlement. Tradition has it that St Augustine preached at Long Compton in about 604 AD as part of his mission to convert England to Christianity.

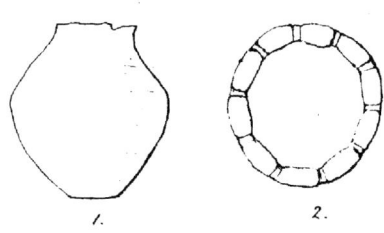

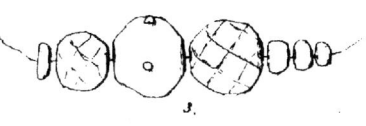

Evidence of people living nearby at this period was found in the mid 19th century when stone quarrying near the Stones revealed an early Saxon cemetery, including typical 6th century grave goods of a cremation urn, beads and a bracelet (right).

In 2015 further finds were made by a group of metal detectorists who reported their discoveries to the local Finds Liaison Officer of the Portable Antiquities Scheme.

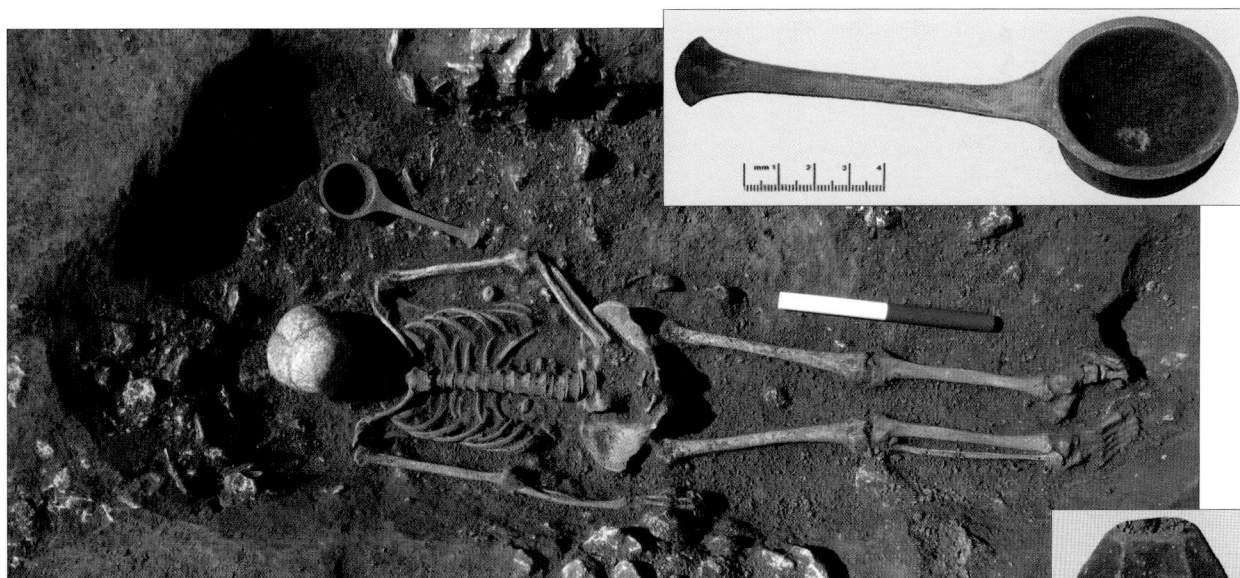

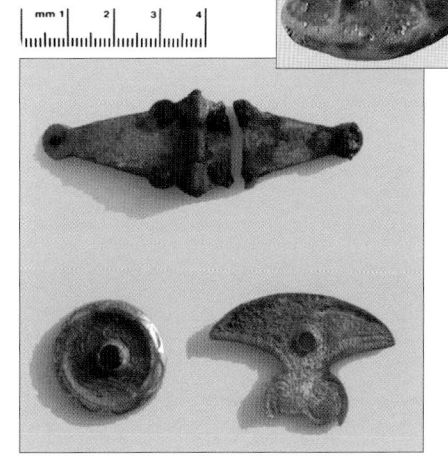

Excavation revealed the grave of a young woman (above) dated to c.620 to 700 AD on the basis of her exceptional grave goods: a long-handled bronze pan, a wooden casket with bronze hinges and silver mounts, a large rock crystal (all right); also two pins with links for a veil or headdress, an antler disc, an amber bead and a dog's tooth (not illustrated). She was clearly an important person.

The cemetery straddles the junction of three parishes (the Rollrights and Long Compton) reflecting the importance of such boundary locations, as well as the attractiveness of the Stones as an ancient sacred meeting place.

A Medieval Estate and its Windmill

The earliest documentary mention of Little Rollright, the parish in which the Stones are located, is in the Domesday Book of AD 1086 (top right). At that time the

manor was worth £5 and was held by Columban the Monk under the tenancy-in-chief of the Bishop of Lincoln. There were 12 villagers, 3 smallholders and 2 slaves. There was land for 6 ploughs and 25 acres of meadow.

During the middle ages Little Rollright was one of the income-generating farming estates of Eynsham Abbey. Like many great Cotswold landowners in the late 15th century, the Abbey saw sheep farming as the way to make money. In two episodes of enclosure in 1496 and 1505, 400 acres of arable were converted to pasture, leading to the decay of five village landholdings and the eviction of 36 tenants. The village never really recovered as a settlement (left).

The boom in wool did not last, and by the 17th century a balance was restored. By the 1590s crops were grown on the well-drained hillside with a post mill for grinding corn on the ridge near the Stones, as shown on Sheldon's tapestry maps and in Camden's *Britannia* (below; p.4).

The Post-medieval and Victorian Landscape

An estate map of c.1690 AD (below) shows the pattern of 17th century landuse and other features of the manorial economy. Crops were grown on the high, well-drained land and animals grazed the steep and undulating hillslopes. Hay meadows occupied the valley floor and there was an area of parkland north of the church. Details of other buildings, triangular fishponds with their sluices, an orchard, hedges and even gates are shown. The Stones were in a small grassy enclave on 'Old Windmill Hill' with a new windmill now further west. Later drawings (eg p.5 and p.7) show that by the early 18th century the large field by the Stones had been subdivided into its current form.

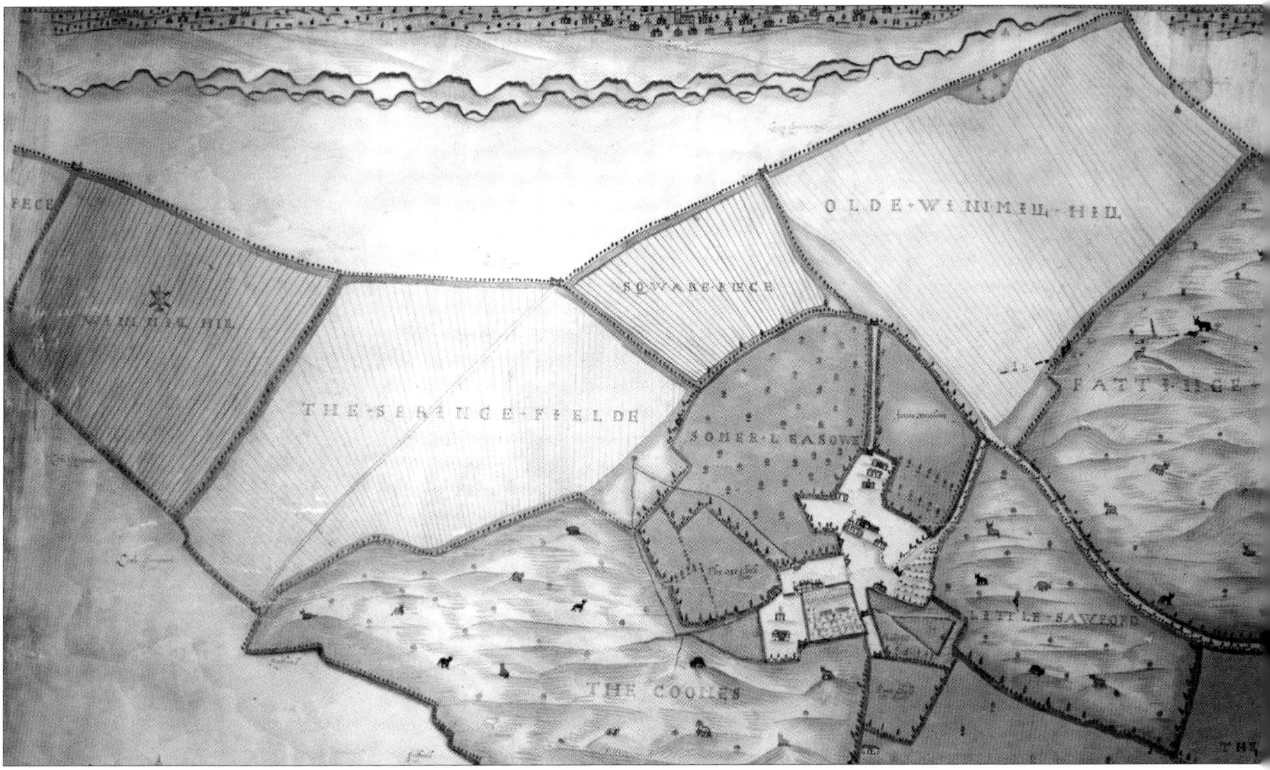

Several fields belonging to the Little Rollright estate were subdivided in the 19th century; and on the north side of the road, the common land of Long Compton was enclosed in 1811.

In the 19th century the owner of Little Rollright planted a ring of larches within the King's Men. The current copses were planted in the 1930s (right).

Royal Signals and Anti-invasion Defence

The prominent location of the Stones on the crest of the Cotswolds means that it is a good vantage point to see in all directions. In 1940, during World War II, the Royal Signals Corps established a post on the natural hillock by the King Stone to watch for enemy aircraft (left). To obtain a clear 360° view, they felled the ring of large old larch trees in the King's Men stone circle.

During the Cold War the post remained part of Britain's defences. In 1961 the simple hut and telephone was upgraded to a Royal Observer Corps early warning post with an underground bunker (below, inset).

The bunker was decommissioned and capped off in 1991. All surface remains were removed (below) but remains of the concrete access shaft are visible nearby.

Geology and Weathering

The Rollright Stones are natural boulders from the basal layer of the local Jurassic oolitic limestone that forms the Cotswold Hills. Their varied thicknesses and shapes reflects variations in the original strata. The rock was laid down on a seabed c.160 million years ago and consists of tiny spherical 'ooliths' and remains of fossilized sea creatures held together by calcium carbonate. Over hundreds of millennia, geological faulting and cycles of erosion and deposition eventually left the boulders exposed on the ground surface within c.500 m of the site.

Stukeley described the stones as *"corroded like worm-eaten wood by the harsh jaws of time"* - the result of weathering over millions of years before the stones were used to build the monuments. The most pitted surfaces would have been uppermost, the chemical effects of rainwater and plant roots etching out crevices in the limestone. In some cases holes were created through the stones (top left).

Weathering has continued since the Stones were erected. A hollow about 30 mm deep with an overhanging lip in the top of one of the King's Men entrance stones is a *kamenitza* typical of limestone exposed to rainwater weathering (below). It indicates a rate of erosion of about 0.75 to 1 mm per century. Such erosion may explain why the leaning portal stones of the Whispering Knights do not touch the central slab on which they may once have rested (left). Surface flaking of various stones shows how frost damage has also played a part.

Lichens and Other Wildlife

The Rollright Stones form an ideal habitat for over 70 kinds of lichen, creating an colourful natural patchwork on the surface of the stones from subtle greys to vibrant yellows (right). Including inconspicuous crust-like species, they completely cover the Stones. The age of some lichens can be estimated by comparing their size with specimens growing on datable stones (like gravestones). One of the oldest (on one of the King's Men entrance stones) may be 800 years old (below).

Attractive wildflowers growing on and around the Stones include the goldilocks buttercup (right) and the rue-leaved saxifrage (bottom right). The hedges beside the path to the Whispering Knights and along the road by the King Stone are ancient parish boundaries with many native species, including field maple and hazel. Predatory birds seen at the site include ravens, buzzards and kites, while song birds include skylarks, yellowhammers and robins (below left).

Management and Conservation

The Rollright Stones are protected by law. They were placed in state Guardianship in 1883 and 1894, and since then additional areas have been added to the Scheduled Ancient Monument. The King's Men and the Whispering Knights are owned by the Rollright Trust; the King Stone by the nearby farm. The Trust leases other land round the Stones and manages the whole complex for public benefit.

The Rollright Trust's priorities are *first,* to ensure a beneficial landuse regime for the physical preservation of the site; *second,* to maintain public access and enhance understanding; and *third,* to enable groups and individuals to make use of the site in ways that are meaningful to present day needs.

Events are regularly held for the summer and winter solstices and other prehistoric festivals (right). The site has been used to exhibit modern sculptures including Anish Kapoor's *Turning the World Inside Out* in 2003 (top left) and for drama productions and TV. The Stones are also regularly used for private wedding and naming ceremonies and other celebrations.

Between 2005 and 2007 the Trust improved access by leasing additional land (below left), dealing with visitor erosion, installing wheelchair accessible gates and paths, and restoring eroded ground profiles round the Whispering Knights and the King Stone. Repairs of damage to the Stones (both accidental and deliberate) are carried out by English Heritage. In recent years this has included stone repairs and paint removal (below right).

Astronomy

The Stones do not exhibit any definite ancient astronomical alignments: the King Stone is not an astronomical outlier of the stone circle; the centre of the King's Men is not (quite) aligned with equinoctial sunrises over the Whispering Knights; and the rough orientation of the stone circle's entrance towards the southern-most setting position of the moon is also of doubtful significance.

But if the Stones have no special archaeo-astronomical interest, the night sky is still a vital part of their setting. Other aspects of their surroundings (the road, fields, vegetation) are much altered compared with prehistory, but along with local landform, the night sky and its constellations are exactly what the people who originally built the Stones experienced.

Nowadays the Stones are highly valued by modern star-gazers through the enthusiastic support of the Chipping Norton Amateur Astronomy Group (CNAAG), who regularly use the site for their own observations and public star-gazing events. In 2012 the Rollright Stones was one of the few places in Britain where the Transit of Venus was observed (below left).

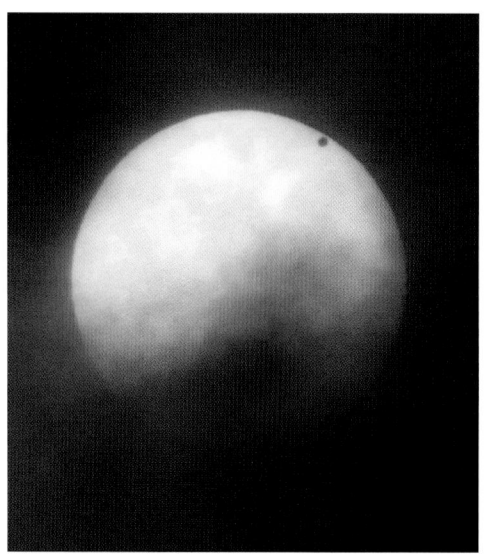

The Stones regularly feature on TV programmes such as *Stargazing Live* and *The Sky at Night,* and in 2014, through the efforts of CNAAG, the Stones were designated a 'Dark Sky Discovery Site', qualifying as 'Orion' class (amongst the darkest publicly accessible venues for stargazing — bottom left). By identifying sites like Rollright where the night sky contributes to their wonder and beauty, the Dark Skies initiative, supported by the Royal Observatories at Greenwich and Edinburgh, the Federation of Astronomical Societies, and the British Astronomical Society, seeks to demonstrate the importance and value of limiting and reversing problems of modern light pollution.

Education and Research

The varied interest of the Rollright Stones, as reflected in the various topics covered in this guidebook, make them an ideal resource for education and research at a variety of levels from primary to higher education. The value of the Stones is not just for learning about or researching the prehistoric past: there is scope to do art and creative writing, geography, maths and science, as well as practical skills.

For schools they are a good introduction to prehistoric monuments of different periods and ideas about what they were for, who built them and how. Primary school visits have become more common since prehistory was introduced into the National Curriculum in 2014, and a programme of activities has been developed. These include:

- A rope timeline that pupils create by attaching labels depicting Rollright history alongside world monuments (top left).
- Stone-moving with levers, sledges and rollers to help understand how the Stones were built, also introducing some practical science as well as requiring good teamwork (right).
- Counting the stones in the stone circle (both children and teachers) statistically showing that they are uncountable !

Other activities include measuring, drawing and painting, role-play, and music.

For older students the Stones have provided fruitful topics for undergraduate and masters' dissertations, which usefully contribute to the Trust's work. These have included visitor surveys (demographic profiles, interests and impressions); a film about Saxon reuse of prehistoric monuments in the Cotswolds; work on how archaeological interpretation of megalithic monuments has evolved; how such ideas relate to practicalities of management and presentation; a pilot App providing digital information for visitors to the Stones; and a short drama for the summer solstice based on some of the legends.

Other independent research initiatives have looked into the role of Sir Norman Lockyer at Rollright (see p.6); further investigation of the Saxon cemetery arising from a metal-detecting find (see p.15); the weathering of limestone (see p.19); and the lichens and plants growing on and around the Stones (see p.20).

Further Reading

The Rollright Stones

Aubrey Burl, 2000 'The Rollright Stones' in *Great Stone Circles: Fables, Fictions, Facts* Yale University Press (reprinted for The Rollright Trust, Banbury)

Thomas Beesley, 1855 'The Rollright Stones' *Trans. N. Oxon. Archaeol. Soc.* **1**, 61-73

William Camden, 1607 *Britannia* (2nd ed.)

Arthur Evans, 1895 'The Rollright Stones and their Folkore', *Folklore* **6**, 6-50

Leslie Grinsell, 1976 *The Rollright Stones and their Folkore,* David and Charles, St Peter Port

George Lambrick, 1988 *The Rollright Stones — Megaliths, Monuments and settlement in the Prehistoric Landscape*, English Heritage Archaeological Report **6**

Jeff Malter and Mark Powell, 2016 The Lichens of the Rollright Stones, *Bulletin British Lichen Society* **No 119** (Winter 2016), 54-66

Percival Oakley Hill, 1894 *A Temple of the Sun: A Guide to the Druidical Remains at Little Rollright*, W. C. Hayes, Chipping Norton

Robert Plot, 1677 *The Natural History of Oxfordshire*

Thomas Ravenhill, 1932 *The Rollright Stones and the Men who Erected Them,* Cornish Bros. (2nd ed)

F C Rickett 2010 *The Rollright Stones History and Legends in Prose and Poetry,* Nabu Press

William Stukeley, 1743 *Abury A Temple of the British Druids, with Some Others, Described,* Innys, Manby, Dod and Brindley, London

Henry Taunt, 1907 *The Rollright Stones, The Stonehenge of Oxfordshire,* H W Taunt and Co, Oxford

Vanessa Winchester, 1988 'An assessment of Lichenometry as a Method for Dating Recent Stone Movements in Two Stone Circles in Cumbria and Oxfordshire' *Botanical Jnl Linnean Soc.* **96** 57–68

The Wider Context of the Stones

Aubrey Burl, 1999 *Great Stone Circles: Fables, Fictions, Facts,* Yale University Press

Aubrey Burl, 2000 *The Stone Circles of Britain, Ireland and Britanny,* Yale University Press

Aubrey Burl, 2005 *Prehistoric Stone Circles,* Shire Books, Princes Risborough (2nd ed)

Aubrey Burl, 2005 *Prehistoric Astronomy and Ritual,* Shire Books, Princes Risborough (2nd ed)

Julian Cope, 1988 *The Modern Antiquarian,* Harper Collins

Timothy Darvill, 2004 *Long Barrows of the Cotswolds and Surrounding Areas,* History Press

Leslie Grinsell, 1976 *Folklore of Prehistoric Sites in Britain*, David and Charles

Ronald Hutton, 1991 *The Pagan Religions of the Ancient British Isles,* Blackwell

Useful Websites

The Rollright Trust: *http://www.rollrightstones.co.uk*

Megalithic Portal: *http://www.megalithic.co.uk*

English Heritage: *http://www.english-heritage.org.uk*

Acknowledgements

I am very grateful to Anni Byard, Ron Dudley-Smith, Mary Edginton, Helena Hamerow, Gill Hey, Meredith Sassoon, David Shirt, Robin Smitten, Sandy Vaughan and Sarah Withey for comments on earlier drafts of this guidebook which have resulted in a number of improvements. I would also like to thank the individuals and institutions who have allowed me to reproduce the images illustrating this booklet as listed overleaf, especially the many who did so free of charge.

Picture Credits

How to Get Involved

DONATIONS

The Rollright Trust does not receive any grants or subsidies from public bodies. As an independent charity we rely for all our funding on entrance charges, event fees and sale of some merchandise – such as this guidebook — together with donations.

VOLUNTEERING

The Trust has no staff or employees but relies on volunteers to act as wardens to welcome visitors, help maintain the site and administer the Trust and its Friends.

BECOMING A FRIEND

The annual subscription (£10/year individual or £15/year family) supports the work of the Trust and entitles Friends to free entry to the site and two newsletters per year, as well as first-hand information and invitations to the Trust's annual Forum and some events at the Stones.

We are always keen to welcome new Friends.

CONTACTING THE TRUST TO GET INVOLVED

If you would like to make a donation, offer your services as a volunteer or support us by becoming a Friend, please do so via the Trust's website at

www.rollrightstones.co.uk/get-involved

THANK YOU